Women and
Super Women

Women and Super Women

JILLY COOPER

With illustrations by
TIMOTHY JAQUES

EYRE METHUEN
LONDON

TO ILSA YARDLEY

With love

First published in 1974
by Eyre Methuen Ltd.
11 *New Fetter Lane, London* EC4P 4EE
Copyright © 1974 *by Jilly Cooper*
Printed in Great Britain by
Butler & Tanner Ltd, Frome and London

ISBN 0 413 32260 2

11.74

Contents

	page
INTRODUCTION	6
The Ages of Women	9
Ladies and Sport	35
The Arts	39
Female Types	43
Women and their Pastimes	67

Introduction

You may ask—not unreasonably—what excuse there can be for adding as much as a jot to the wordy flux that has poured off the presses in the last few years on the subject of the female sex. Can it be that there yet remains a syllable unuttered on the topic of 'unpaid domestic servitude', or some unignited spark of controversy over the locale of the female orgasm?

The Female Ghetto, The Sensuous Eunuch, The Ascent of Women etc. etc.—the only thing these joyless outpourings have in common is a dreary ability to take themselves too seriously and an infinite capacity for grumbling about the female condition.

Only a couple of decades ago there was a universally hummed popular song called *I enjoy being a girl*. Today, in the mid-seventies, Jan Morris was practically lynched for saying the same thing.

In fact in turning from man into woman, Miss Morris has gone very much against the tide, for the most depressing aspect about women today is that so many of them seek to be becoming more and more like men. One sees them wearing trousers the whole time, cutting their hair short, storming the stock exchange and the civil service, taking over men's top jobs, taking the sexual initiative, refusing to do more than a minimum of housework, paying someone else to look after their children.

The hand that is stretching out to rule the world,

seems no longer to have any desire to rock the cradle. Gone are the days when girls were dear little things exclusively manufactured from sugar and spice.

Women, as we knew them, in fact, are a rapidly vanishing phenomenon in grave danger of extinction. Conservationists fretting over the fate of the rhinoceros or the butterfly should immediately turn their attention to rescuing the female, if only to preserve her in Wild Wife Parks or Bird Sanctuaries before it is too late.

I felt it was essential before the sex became extinct or disappeared in a pouffe of smoke to get down on paper details of the female's behaviour pattern, her hobbies, her breeding and brooding habits, and also to categorise the physical characteristics of the various sub-species: nymphomaniacs, Tory ladies, virgins, debutantes, lady cricketers and many more.

The result was *Women and Super Women*. And Timothy Jaques, who did the drawings, and I sincerely hope that this little monograph may be placed beside the dinosaur skeletons in the Natural History Museum, as a memento for future generations of the days when the female sex still roamed the world.

Woman proud woman clad in little briefs. . . . I shall no doubt be accused of being too harsh on my sex. But I would like to protest like Macheath, if perhaps for different reasons, that I love the sex: "Nothing unbends the mind like them."

I am constantly amazed by their beauty, their vulnerability and above all by their intrinsic sillyness even when they are at their most serious and tub-thumping. All women are good, as the proverb says, for something or nothing.

Women and Super Women was written very appropriately in longhand in the pages of a publisher's dummy (a book with blank pages) for *The Gathering Storm* by Winston Churchill.

As we hurtle towards gynocracy, and the strident howls of the Women's Liberationists become more clamorous, I doubt if the battle of the sexes has ever raged more bitterly. But before they take over altogether I think women should perhaps heed Sir Compton Mackenzie's words:

"Women do not find it difficult nowadays to behave like men; but they often find it extremely difficult to behave like gentlemen."

The Ages of Women

SCHOOLGIRLS

Schoolgirls write endless letters to schoolboys scented with Goya's Great Expectations, which progress from Dear to My Very Dear to Darling Darling Darling as the term passes. Status is entirely dependent on how many Valentines they get. A lot of wishbones are wasted on Paul Newman.

During the school term schoolgirls smoke like chimneys but don't inhale, smuggle in pornography and spend a good deal of time asking more sexually experienced pupils: "What's it like, what's it really like?"

During the holidays they lie on the floor, play pop music too loudly for their parents' liking, and keep transistors under the bedclothes so they can listen to Capital Radio all night. A lot of time is spent reading beauty advice books about not squeezing blackheads and drinking P.L.J. Occasionally they make out lists of every part of their body, and launch heroic campaigns to make each part more beautiful.

Schoolgirls are supposed to be filled to the brim with girlish glee, but are actually permanently in despair because there is no possibility of Paul Newman or anyone else who looks like him ever loving them back. Meanwhile Paul Newman and thousands of men who look like him are having fantasies about nubile schoolgirls.

TEENAGERS

Teenagers have spots, puppy fat, immortal longings, sleep all day, and worry about kissing properly, whether they're exchanging too much saliva or going on too long, or whether they should be stroking the back of their boyfriend's neck as they do in films. When they first progress to French kissing all they can think of is how disgusting the underneath of men's tongues feels.

All teenagers live in jeans with mottoes embroidered all over them, which are evidently a great icebreaker: you read each other's private parts and suddenly you're friends. To quote from one teenage magazine:

"He had *Beauty is Truth* down one side of his jeans and *Abandon all hope ye* on the crutch and the sort of smile that labelled him a very real person."

Most teenagers are very keen on someone called Mousy Tongue.

They change at least three times a day, and spend three hours on their faces before coming downstairs, in the hope that one of their father's friends will chat them up, or a group of workmen will whistle at them in the street. They also stuff Kleenex into their bras, giggle a lot, spend all their money on *Movie Magazine*, *Jackie* and pop records, and wonder why they can't marry Paul Newman. After all, Juliet was married at fourteen, wasn't she? Permanently Spock-marked, they believe the world owes them a living, and stay in jobs only three weeks.

Other occupations are slamming doors, having wild parties when their parents are away, smashing crockery from pre-menstrual tension and pinching their mothers' clothes.

"She's got a man, and she's past it, what does she need with clothes anyway?"

To get their revenge, mothers often hang around when their daughters have friends in, cramping everyone's style when they want to neck and talk about sex.

Teenagers are also intensely irritated by their parents continually grumbling about money, but still spending fortunes on drink.

VIRGINS

Per Ardor ad Asterisks.

Almost a collector's item these days. Virginity is supposed to be something you give your husband like engraved cuff-links on your wedding day.

When I was a gel girls kept fantastically quiet if they lost their virginity, now they get panicky if they haven't lost it by the time they're twenty-one.

Virgins are permanently under siege from Herrick urging them to gather rosebuds, which is a euphemism for losing it. They worry that once they've lost IT they're going to want IT all the time. They know they're saving IT for something, but are terrified that it's getting too late, and soon, no one's going to want IT. Virgins also worry about the pain on

"What d'you mean—lost it?"

their wedding night, but so much will be going on, rockets exploding, asterisks, the breaking of waves and Ravel's Bolero in the background, that they'll be completely distracted from any pain.

Girls who have lost their virginity often move to other parts of the country so they can pretend to be virgins again.

One's mother and one's daughters are always virgins and have children by internal combustion.

DEBS

Red Eyes at night, Deb's delight.

Debs live in the General Trading Company, are all called Fiona and Georgina, wear headscarves on the chin to keep their mouths from falling open, have high clipped little voices, never dye their hair and fornicate like stoats. They also wear trousers that don't fit, carry Gucci bags with another scarf attached to the handle and wear flat shoes with tongues and chains.

Much of their time is spent grumbling to the newsagent that the latest copy of the *Tatler* hasn't come in, eating their way through five-course charity dinners in aid of the starving, and working as "sekketries" in offices, where they get on surprisingly well because they talk to everyone in an attempt to prove that only the middle classes treat the lower classes badly.

In ten years' time, their hair will be tucked inside a petalled hat, red veins will be springing on their cheeks, and they'll be wearing exactly the same clothes that were fashionable when they were Debs.

FLATSHARERS

You tend to see them most on Fridays, again with suitcases clutched in their hot little hands as they surge towards bus stops in South Kensington and Knightsbridge, on their way to offices where most of them work as rather imperfect typists.

On the bus they will shout across to one another about "Dominic and Gideon and those two perfectly super medical students we met skiing."

Their suitcases, which block the cubby-hole under the stairs, contain a week's dirty washing for Mummy and a smart little dress in case there's a drinks party, or a smart long dress in case there's a hunt ball. Most of the weekend will be spent sleeping off the rigors of the week: a week of jousting for men, gossiping with other girls, rowing because Samantha hasn't cleaned the frying pan, and eating scant suppers off big knees in front of hired television sets.

These are the Guardswomen of S.W.3. London is the battleground and men are the prizes. Here in bathrooms festooned with drying bras and tights that drip like some Chinese torture, they will soothe their battered minds and bodies in tepid water from some rusty boiler that would put Heath Robinson to shame.

Here they will sleep in a bedroom not unlike the dorm at school. They have come to London because they've been told that is where the action is—most of them are a little bewildered to find they aren't having a more madly gay time.

Girls who share flats seldom have much in common except a desire to find a mate. They probably came together in the first place because two of them went to the same school, or their mothers did, and a third or fourth were needed to pay the rent.

Fed on a diet of *Woman's Own* and Barbara Cart-horse, much of their time is spent reading their horoscopes or wishing on the New Moon: "Oh find me a husband, a Prince Charming to whisk me away from this Squalor to St James, Spanish Place."

Men visiting the flat are seldom allowed in the bedroom, not out of modesty, but because they would be so appalled by the mess: clothes everywhere, spilt make-up, a week's supply of coffee cups gathering dust under the bed. And yet from this squalor, elegant and beautiful girls will regularly issue forth for the cocktail party round.

Then there are those fiendish flat dinner parties, when the candles burn down and the ill-assorted guests, a farmer, a male model and a stockbroker, are forced to make stilted conversation until a revolting dinner that wouldn't disgrace the Borgias is served up three hours late.

But there are good moments: setting off for the fray in a shared taxi, which smells like a summer garden from everyone's scent, or those manic sessions at two o'clock in the morning when you all come back a bit tight from different outings and shriek about your experiences, until the old boot in the flat below starts tapping on the ceiling.

And it's somewhere to live even if the rent is high and the landlady's a nosy old bag, and you can always find a new flat or new flat-mates. For the Guardswomen of Chelsea have one aim in life, they're looking for a husband as hard as the landlady is looking for the rent.

FIANÇAYS: TROUSSEAU'S CONFESSIONS

"Orange blossom is quite the Fox's brush of Female life."

SURTEES

The Fiançay can be forgiven for being a little smug. From the age of four she's been worrying about whether she's going to get married or not; now the Beechers Brook of her life has been cleared. The temptation, however, is very strong to kick her in the teeth as she sits about holding her hands in such a position that everyone notices the sapphire set in two diamonds flashing on her finger, beginning every

15

sentence 'Gideon says', and lecturing her unmarried friends on the inefficiency of their sex lives.

"Daddy says I must be vacant to get engaged."

Her smugness will be short-lived, she will be far too busy in the weeks before the wedding making lists, writing thank you letters, being photographed for the *Tatler* with a soppy expression on her face, dragooning bridesmaids into frightful dresses and coping with their tantrums afterwards, coping with her father's tantrums because none of the younger generation are answering invitations, and worrying that senile Uncle Willy will expose himself at the reception.

She will also be looking drawn from pre-wedding crash diets, practising wedding night shrieks and praying that Gideon will believe that story about her losing her virginity on the tennis court.

It's to be a quiet wedding with eight hundred guests, three bus-loads of tenants, and 'Sheep may Safely Graze' at the entrance of the bride.

NEWLY WEDS

"YOUNG WIFE: *I've been trying to figure out where my husband spends his evenings. Last night I came home early, and there he was.*" JACK HULBERT

Newly weds are pretty smug when not collapsing from exhaustion. Supposed to look dewy but usually have bits of sleep rather than stars in their eyes. Spend their lunch hours shopping and struggling home with bulging carrier bags, which usually collapse just as they're getting out of the tube.

"We've only been married four weeks two days and five minutes," they say with a coy giggle. "We still celebrate our weekiversaries."

Up until now people have referred to them as Honor and Norm; now they'll be called the Longbottoms, or the Cheviots, like a range of mountains.

WIVES

Wilt! Thou hast this woman for thy wedded wife.

When a man asks if he can bring his wife, you can be sure she's a beauty or a battleaxe, he's either proud of her or too scared to leave her behind.

Super Woman is perfection as a wife, her house is always spotless, her husband's shirts laundered at home, "because the laundry do them so badly". Although she does a full-time job, she is able to give intimate little dinners for her husband's business clients once or twice a week, type out his reports, watch his calorie intake, rev up in gold lamé every night in bed, yet be up to cook his breakfast, and hand him his briefcase and umbrella as he sets out for work. All her girl friends detest her.

"My husband only has eyes for me," she says smugly. Eyes maybe; presumably the sensible fellow keeps his member for someone else.

Super Woman is always flirting with her husband in front of other people. It looks bad: as Oscar Wilde says, rather like washing one's clean linen in public.

UNHAPPY WIVES
"The best part of married life is the fights. The rest is merely so-so" THORNTON WILDER

Unhappy wives have dreadful clothes. What with school fees and Norman's philandering, they can't afford to buy any new ones.

"She's let herself go dreadfully," say her friends, then add mystifyingly, "What she really ought to do is really let herself go, and find a lover."

"I'm letting myself go—goodbye!"

The marriage is now in injury time, each party in its separate hell; the only sexual kick the couple get is out of rowing with each other. They always talk about having "stuck together because of the children", as though the little blighters have been using glue and sellotape on them.

FIRST WIVES

People tell me snakes are not dangerous to handle, and that they are not slimy but cool and dry, but my flesh still creeps when I see them. It's as impossible to expect a second wife to like a first wife, as it is a wife to like a mistress. The latter will always be a threat, albeit an imaginary one, to the former. And yet curiosity draws them together. Women who love the same man have a kind of bitter Freemasonry.

When first wives meet up with their first husbands they annoy the second wife by indulging in an orgy of name-swapping about people they knew in the old days.

One first wife, when she sends her children to stay with the second wife, includes a list of their clothing to be ticked off like a school list when they come home.

Other than praising her children, the quickest way to endear oneself to a woman is to say diabolical things about her husband's first wife.

STEPMOTHERS

An archetypal bitch, the most unpleasant character in literature, who visits all the imagined sins of the first wife on any of the first wife's children. Can often be seen at cocktail parties grumbling: "Of course, Gideon refuses to see any of her faults, but what can you expect with a mother like that."

Stepmothers alas are here to stay, because even though the concept of the large family is declining, it flourishes in other directions: "Well, Gideon's got three fiends from a previous marriage," you'll hear a wife saying. "And I've got three angels from when I was living with Alaster, and Gideon and I've got two between us, so there's quite a crowd at weekends."

Someone should write a saga of the seventies called the 39 steps.

Third wives usually get on very well with first wives.

Fourth wives usually get on very well with second wives.

PREGNANT WOMEN

The pregnant woman is supposed to have a glow about her and to have never looked better. A fantasy built up by women's magazines. In fact she's a write-off from the sex appeal point of view after the fourth month, a sort of neuter, who wears her dresses eighteen inches higher at the front than the back— dresses she expects to wear afterwards as "little tops", whereas in fact they are more like the Big Top, or a marquee that could house the whole neighbourhood.

Pregnant women sit with their legs apart and have swollen ankles, which is probably what is meant by pregnant paws. Most of them are in love with their gynaecologist, and spend their time feeling their babies kicking like full-backs.

Plain women like being pregnant because suddenly they become 'interesting' and men, terrified they're going to explode, treat them like Dresden. Many women seem to believe there is some merit in suffering, and disapprove of any pain-killing methods. One woman I know insisted the midwife left the door open so her husband could hear her screams and know what she was going through.

If a woman gets pregnant immediately after she's had a baby, everyone clicks their tongues and blames the husband for being a dirty beast who couldn't leave her alone.

Sexual Norm's wife Honor is in a complete muddle; her friends come forward with an avalanche of advice on looking after the baby, all conflicting. The battle rages between the bottle boilers and the non-boilers, disposable nappies, Harrington towels, the Nappy Service and kidney-shaped safety-pins. Everyone gives her wildly differing lists on what she'll need. Sexual Norm thinks a Layette is a very small Nymphomaniac.

Honor tries to read baby books, but the page always falls open at vomiting or green motions. Sexual Norm enjoys the section on the Husband's Reactions: "It says I'm going to feel very left out," he reads happily. "And be grumpy towards you and spend more evenings with men friends and flirting with other women."

"Three safety pins, a marble and about 50p in loose change, and you said he wasn't eating."

LOVELY YOUNG MOTHERS

Milton, thou should be sterilising at this hour.

Young mothers have sick on their shoulders, go round with bags of equipment like plumbers, sigh continually, have very long ears from listening out for crying, and look as though they haven't slept for weeks, which is true. They spend their time pinching their babies to see if they're awake, and crying into the washing machine. They sterilise everything and would sterilise their husbands if they could.

Most women fancy the concept of themselves as lovely young mothers. As a girl friend of mine once said: "There was I with Tarquin and Crispin on my knee, hoping she'd say what a lovely picture the three of us made—and she didn't."

UNMARRIED MOTHERS

"You don't think Jennifer'll do anything foolish?"
"Oh she's always doing foolish things."

Supposed to be the heroine of our time. She is now called a one-parent family. People say quite untruthfully that there is no stigma attached to being an unmarried mother. Actually she can't win. If she goes out to work people accuse her of depriving her child of its only source of affection, if she stays at home she's accused of living off the state, and the social security ladies come nosy-parkering round looking for thick woollen socks and Y-fronts on the clothes line.

It is only easy to be an unmarried mother if you can afford a nanny and a lover.

Unmarried mothers, according to their mothers, always get pregnant the *first* time they sleep with a man. They have a bitter look like women prisoners, live in hostels, and are understandably hostile. Married women sometimes employ them as nannies, automatically assuming they'll be wildly grateful, then start worrying that the unmarried mother will favour her own child rather than the employer's children.

BARREN LADIES

Women who can't have children worry continually that their in-laws and parents will develop complexes about being a grandchildless couple. They are also terrified of getting a dog in case people assume it is a child substitute.

Trying to have babies is a most dismal process. Most infertile women have worn a furrow down Harley Street, picketing gynaecologists, having five D and Cs, four salpingograms, and 500 cwt of ironmongery inside them. There is also the tedious busi-

23

ness of taking one's temperature every day, and then having to pounce on each other when it goes up, which is always the morning you're late for work, or suffering from debilitating hangovers, or simply not fancying each other. Then a fortnight later, getting wildly excited because the curse is half an hour late, then feeling like committing suicide when it finally arrives.

If you ask a woman at a party if she's got any children she either says No—and there'll be a long embarrassed pause before she adds: "But I've got lots of godchildren, and I adore my five little nieces." Or she'll say no, then add hastily, "But we've only been married eighteen months."

If you can't produce children, people automatically assume you're undersexed. Society on the whole is quite sympathetic, but on the other hand rigidly disapproves of couples who can have children, but choose not to. Everyone will chunter disapprovingly about "selfishness" every time they eat out in a restaurant, buy a picture, or take another holiday abroad.

Super Woman is always giving herself heirs.

MISTRESSES—THE OTHER WOMAN

SHE: *Are you sure your wife won't mind about us?*
HE: *You'd better be careful, she's already killed five ladies and one platinum blonde.* EXECUTIVE SUITE

At one time kept in back streets, now flaunted in posh restaurants, mistresses have smooth marbly limbs, fur counterpanes and mirrors on the ceiling.

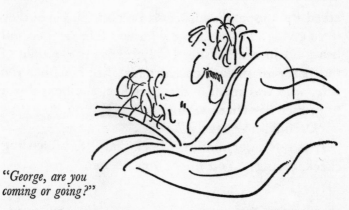

"George, are you coming or going?"

They also carry chisels and hammers to prise their lover loose from his wife.

Mistresses always say they're having an affair with a married man not a husband, and then add: "His wife's frightfully unattractive, a bit 'com' too; he's done so well since he married her, but she hasn't 'grown' with him."

The Kept Woman is usually the well kept woman, frightened of growing old and losing her figure. She complains: "I've given him the bust years of my life."

Her life consists of lunches, a few stolen hours after work, everything quick, nervy and watch-checking. She seldom gets her lover to stay over. Come midnight, he's out of her flat like a shot. He's probably frightened of seeing himself first thing in the morning in that overhead mirror.

Mistresses are always free at Christmas and Easter and are at a loose end at weekends, but, alas, loose is the last thing they get the opportunity to be.

One couple I know decided to be civilised and

25

asked the husband's mistress to a cocktail party they were giving. The mistress, who was tall, slender and beautiful in a deathshead way, chose the middle of the party to make her entrance. Approaching the wife, who was small and terrier-like, she bent down to proffer her cheek saying:

"Darling, how lovely."

A second later she leapt back, hand to a bleeding cheek, crying: "You bitch, you bit me."

GAY DIVORCÉES

"No desire to get married—it would take an awful lot of butter to get me into the frying pan again." GYPSY ROSE LEE.

You're only middle-aged once.

Gay divorcées wear big hats, gold pants, dark glasses and diamonds big as glacier mints. They have cleavages like the Grand Canyon, roulette chips rattling round at the bottom of their bags, and have never done it in the back of anything except a Rolls Royce.

They're just the sort of women to get schoolboys through A level Sex, and about whom Oscar Wilde said: "She has at least a dozen pasts and they all fit."

Gay divorcées never have to buy their own scent, and have voluptuous figures upholstered in black net—sort of mattresses en titre.

BEAUTIFUL DESERTED WOMEN

> Born in Hazlemere
> Schooled at Cheltenham
> Courted in Kensington
> Married in Chelsea
> Bliss in Fulham
> Parted in Tears
> Divorced in Putney

Putney is teeming with beautiful deserted women rattling round in seven-bedroom houses, with two or three children. They have a forlorn air about them like a glove hanging on a hawthorn tree—no good without a partner. Most of them are impossibly overworked, going out to a job every day, coping single-handed with all the bills and mortgages, bringing up the children, and having to stay home from work jeopardising their jobs if one of the children is sick.

Their friends say tactless things like: "Henry's getting a bit spoilt, he needs a man about the house."

Meanwhile Henry's father takes him out at weekends, and returns him loaded with presents, nevertheless claiming he can't afford 50p. a week more alimony.

Other friends say Poor Honor's going through a very bad Patch, as though she were having trouble with a naughty mongrel.

It is very difficult these days for deserted women to get married again unless they break up a marriage. Unattached men in their thirties—apparently emasculated by the demands of Women's Lib and the

27

emancipation of women generally—either seek the company of dollybirds who look up to them, or go queer out of spite.

As a modern novel said recently, "We've lost more men to homosexuality than we ever did in two world wars."

"I've been deserted."

The beautiful deserted woman is usually asked to dinner parties to make up the numbers with a queer or someone's husband down from the north. When men take her out they assume she must be screaming for it, as she's been used to regular sex. It is almost impossible for her to refuse to sleep with men—she's not given a second virginity to save for her second marriage, and if she says no, men go storming off into the night in a huff.

MAIDEN AUNT, MAIDEN ENGLAND

"On the occasions when Aunt is calling to Aunt like masta-dons bellowing across primeval swamps and Uncle James' letter about Cousin Basil's peculiar behaviour is being shot

round the family circle—(Please read this carefully and pass on to Jane)—the family have a tendency to ignore me."
P. G. WODEHOUSE

Aunts are the salt of the earth; they're close enough for you to tell them things that would shock or hurt your parents. When you're about sixteen they ask you to call them by their Christian names. Awful women ask their friends' children to call them Auntie.

At weddings older aunts wear pull-on felts and wedding-cake crumbs on their moustaches and charge round spraying incesticide on any relations who get the least bit familiar.

BACHELOR GIRLS

"A woman with fair opportunities and without a positive hump may marry whom she likes." THACKERAY

People always assume that bachelors are single by choice and spinsters because nobody asked them. It never enters their heads that poor bachelors might have worn the knees of their trousers out proposing to girls who rejected them or that a girl might deliberately stay unmarried because she didn't want to spend the rest of her life filling a man's stomach with food and washing his dirty shirts.

Invariably bachelor girls are referred to by their families as Poor Norma or Poor Honor, and one can understand why they go home so seldom, when their parents' eyes are so full of questions they daren't ask.

If a girl gets married too young, everyone assumes she's pregnant, or the marriage will break up in a few weeks, or she's such a rabbit she can't wait until

29

she's older for regular sex. Between twenty and twenty-six is quite acceptable for a girl to be still single; after that parents get a bit shelf-conscious, and start saying defensively: "Jennifer hasn't got time to think of marriage, she's got this very important job at the Ministry—absolutely J.B.'s right-hand man."

In a few years' time they will be hinting that J.B.'s relationship with their daughter isn't quite so platonic.

"I know if J.B. weren't quite so devoted to his children he and Jennifer . . ."

Then J.B. leaves his wife and elopes with a guardsman, which blows that one sky high.

An awareness of their parents' desire to get them married and the sight of all their girl friends with husbands and children often panics single women in their late 20s or early 30s into disastrous marriages. This is a vital time not to lose one's cool. It seems unfair, though, that so many women get divorced and remarried a number of times; and some of us don't get a chance at all.

When women get married over thirty they seldom wear white—it somehow doesn't seem fitting to flaunt one's lack of experience.

MOTHER-IN-LAW

"Behind every successful man, there's an astonished mother-in-law." RICHARD NIXON

Princess Anne's got married, so they've got to make do with you.

The great mistake with a future mother-in-law is to assume she must be lovely to have produced anyone as lovely as 'him'. You roll up starry-eyed to meet her, forgetting that for her you're just the end of a string of girl friends, and she doesn't like your pedal pushers and sequinned shirt worn to impress his teenage sister, and your hips (because he likes you thin) aren't childbearing enough.

'She'll be extravagant," she's probably thinking. "Will she cook and mend and watch his weight, will she be the sort who rushes back to work the moment she has a baby?"

One of the troubles after marriage is that mothers-in-law only meet daughters-in-law when one of them is absolutely dead with exhaustion. When the mother-in-law comes to stay, the daughter-in-law sweats her guts out bulling up the house, trying to prove to her mother-in-law that she's keeping her son in the style to which he's accustomed. Then the mother-in-law arrives two hours early to find the house in chaos, the joint not in the oven and the children in their pyjamas.

Equally, when one goes to stay with one's mother-in-law she's absolutely knackered cleaning out spare bedrooms and cooking for five days ahead.

"I've run out of animals," said my mother-in-law despairingly, wondering what on earth to feed my husband's sister and her family on after they'd been staying a week.

Don't be misled by the fact your husband bitches about his family. That's his privilege, and he won't be amused if you do the same yourself.

Learn to play bridge, said one woman's magazine, the hardest rind conceals the sweetest fruit.

THE CHANGE OF LIFE

They're changing lives at Buckingham Palace.

Men are always supposed to be the nicer sex, because they get on so much better together than women do, but I think it's a miracle any women are on speaking terms at all, as fifty per cent of the time one of them will be suffering from pre-menstrual tension.

As my housekeeper says, God was in a cranky mood when he made women, what with the curse, childbirth pains, post-natal gloom, pre-menstrual tension, all sorts of gynaecological capers, and finally the change of life as a last act, and not all that well written at that.

How old is she? people ask. About thirty-seven, comes the answer, and everyone nods knowingly, and mutters, The Change.

"Maurice—I think I've started the change."

Must be hell, all those hot flushes like geysers in New Zealand, drenched sheets and going red as a radish. It's not much compensation either, the way women's magazines are always rabbiting on about not having to take the pill any more, and the joys of mature sex, and the quiet serenity of the older woman.

The mother's change of life often coincides with her daughter's adolescence, but the daughter invariably gets blamed for being difficult.

Women going through the change of life often pretend their daughters are older than they are so people will gasp, and say: "You couldn't possibly have a daughter that age. I thought you were sisters."

OLD LADIES

Old ladies live with other older ladies whom they bully shamelessly, not because they need a companion but a sparring partner.

Rich old ladies drench themselves in lavender water, and at Christmas their relations subject them to arselick and old lace in the hope of inheriting some cash.

Poverty-stricken old ladies have a frightful time, sitting with only one bar of the fire on, and buying dog scraps from the butcher for a dog they don't possess. They do have some compensations, they can travel free on buses, and if they live alone in Camden Town they are entitled to a free budgerigar.

The real poverty in fact is in ourselves. For not looking after them better.

WORKING WIVES

Usually filled to the brim with resentment, encouraged by their mothers, who keep saying "You must

"Dog's got in again, Mum."

get so tired darling, and why doesn't Norm ask for a rise?"

If a man leaves his wife and goes off with another woman and his wife is not working, society blames her for becoming a cabbage and getting bogged down with domesticity; If she is working they blame her for neglecting her husband and not providing him with hot dinners.

Ladies and Sport

CRICKETERS

Women cricketers have divided skirts, long white socks, heaving aertex bosoms, broken fingernails, and spend their time emitting raucous cries of: "Well stopped, Daphne."

"Wide? What d'you mean *wide?"*

All have names like Whoopsy Daisy and drive sports cars. They are a disgrace. A friend of mine once described Tampax as a long stop between two short legs.

"Straighten those arms and let's get our tummy off the floor, shall we?"

KEEP FIT LADIES

Have black semicircles underneath the armpits of their blue denim shirts and don't get enough sex at home. Oh fit white lady who nobody loves.

LADY ATHLETES

Are pumped full of drugs and have strong sinewy legs. If you produce a dildo or a vibrator, they will attempt to run relay races with it.

HORSEY GIRLS—WHEN LOVELY WOMAN STOOPS TO FILLY

Go to any stables or horse show and you will find a Humbert Humbert's paradise: hordes of nubile girls wearing boots, expressions of innate superiority, and staggeringly tight breeches, their mousy hair rippling down their backs. Slightly bolshy, they would rather muck out than muck in. Most of them are in love with Graham Fletcher, and less snooty than they look. They never talk about anything but

36

horses and take Equi-Librium to stop themselves getting over-excited.

"Well, I think it should be called the chest stroke, Charlene."

SWIMMERS

All called Little Nan Ray, they have oiled muscular shoulders, no busts, one-piece bathing dresses, run to fat and are touched up by disgusting old coaches in white flannels with watches round their necks. They also have bloodshot eyes, separated eyelashes, smell of chlorine and blow their noses in the water with their hands. When it comes to marriage they have no difficulty in taking the plunge.

RUGGER WIVES

Deserve a chapter in Foxe's *Book of Martyrs*. If they're not washing rugger shirts and having their best suitcases stolen to accommodate revolting towels and rugger boots, they're freezing on the touchline crying Come on Company, their faces turning purple and

37

red like a mandrill's bottom. Alternatively, they can spend all afternoon chopping lettuce, and scraping paste made from prawns and other fish on sliced bread and marge, and bitching about the other wives who haven't turned up to spread.

Later they're expected to make a warm half of beer last all evening—even if you wash shorts, you're not allowed to drink them. Rugger wives more than anybody have mastered the art of sweating out a drink.

They don't have sex on Friday night, because their husband is keeping his eye, if nothing else, in, or on Saturday because he'll be too drunk.

Much of her time will be spent answering team secretaries (when her husband is two-timing his own team by playing for some other team with a ludicrous name like The Wasps), and saying most unconvincingly that her husband's been away on business all week, and won't be back from the trip until after kick-off on Saturday.

Newly weds usually come every week to Rugger matches during the first year, and say Gideon's wonderful, he never puts it in crooked. After that they turn up less and less frequently.

Super Woman always breezes in with two featherlight sponges filled with butter icing and asks if she can have the tin back. Everything would be very different if all rugger players looked like David Duckham.

The Arts

"Haven't you got any jeans, dear?"

LADY MUSICIANS

L'Après midi d'un phoney

There are no women of genius, they are all men. A statement borne out by Virginia Woolf's description of Dame Ethel Smyth rehearsing in "A short skirt, a workmanlike jersey, a battered felt hat, a flat chest, a drip on the end of her nose, and a powerful baritone voice, echoing through Portland Place."

Lady instrumentalists ride the cello sidesaddle, toss their heads a lot, and are inclined to be scruffy. Opera singers run to fat, and embarrass their children by singing Wagner in what they imagine to be sotto voce on station platforms. The only compensation is you can never hear the words.

ACTRESSES

Worry continually about bad breath, spend their

time resting and can never be rung up before lunch-time. They seldom have parts of either kind; "there is no work about", and most actors are queer.

LADY NOVELISTS

Good listeners because they're always on the look-out for copy. They justify their nosiness by saying it was Proust's curiosity that made him a great writer.

Lady novelists usually wear too much face powder so it clogs in the cleft of their noses, lipstick on their collars, and biro marks on their pillows and dresses. They are no good at sustaining relationships with men, but this is all to the good because every ghastly let-down is the silver lining of being able to write about it afterwards.

"*Before the Police arrive I think you ought to tell me all about it.*"

Mixing often with queers, they are sustained by syrup of fags. They have large bottoms from sitting down so much, untidy houses, and seldom use a hair-brush or have varicose veins.

They are often found in bookshops surreptitiously moving their own books up to the top of the pile. They keep going to the loo at parties not because of weak bladders but merely to feed their nosy parking metres, and write down the latest witticism on the back of their cheque books.

When they tell you who they are, you've never heard of them. They pretend to have been very unhappy at school.

ARTISTS

Lady painters are mostly members of the behind the door school. Should stick to painting their faces.

ARTISTES

Sing 'Pale Hands I Loved' at geriatric concerts.

STUDENTS

Crinkly hair, college scarves, hunched shoulders, with so many chips on you get splinters if you pounce on them. Tend to fall in love with one-sonnet-a-year poets, who they fiercely defend as geniuses, wash their hair once a month, and have cats with hysterical names out of the classics, and posters on their walls of two hands coming out of the lavatory. Later they become Graduates and wonder if it was all worth it.

GRADUATES

Never capture the first fine careless rapture when they were the toast of L.M.H. Particularly in Oxford and Cambridge where the men outnumber the girls, they get an inflated idea of their own sex appeal and often marry very attractive men out of their own sexual hierarchy. Marriages which break up later.

Having graduated they find to their horror that they have been prepared to do precisely nothing, and after taking a typing course which is far more of a headache to them than a school leaver of sixteen, they get a job in publishing at a thousand pounds a year.

They have a permanent air of not being wanted, which is true. The only thing for them to do is to take other degrees, grumble and despise other women who aren't graduates. In their houses are rush mattings, and copies of the *T.L.S.* and the *Listener* unread.

Sometimes they resort to gardening and cooking, which is as far as their creativity will stretch.

Kinsey quotes that between fifty and eighty per cent of academic women never achieve sexual satisfaction, so they're a bit cross about that too.

Female Types

"Mr. Foster, I never cross my bridges until they eventuate."

DUMB BLONDES

"How do you manage to do so many silly things in one day?"
"I get up early."

Like sex symbols, dumb blondes are out of fashion today. In the old days they had huge busts, and said things like: "Oh look, that seagull's just excruciated on the deck."

Now most of them are brunettes who have lost all their exuberance, keep their cool, never utter, and get a reputation for being mysterious, which men erroneously believe will lead to frenzied fanatical bedroom payoffs.

JEWISH MOTHERS

Beyond reproach, since they've given the world so many marvellous people. Tend to be a bit overpossessive. A Jewish girl friend of mine told me she and her husband had made love on the bathroom floor the other night. "How romantic," I said, "after you've been married ten years." "We can't screw in the bed," she said. "Daniel sleeps with us."

Daniel is five.

LANDLADIES

Premises. Premises.

TORY LADIES

Wear petalled hats in summer and pull-on felts in winter; have ringing voices, grey short perms, open pores, closed minds, refer to the lower classes as 'them', but consider themselves very democratic because "I get on awfully well with my Mrs G." Their Mrs Gs refer to them behind their backs as "bossy boots". They're always talking about "approaching the mayor or the local tradesmen", as though they're going to sidle up and tweak them on the nose.

Much of their time is spent waving tins at street corners and giving long sentences. They have flat bottoms from sitting on so many committees, and flat feet, for trampling on people. (They wouldn't want anyone to escape under the arches.) When they go shopping they pull baskets on wheels with copies of the *Daily Telegraph* inside.

TRENDY LEFTIES: NON-U-TOPIA

Radical chicks. Always getting up petitions, and

organising community centres with their own theatre workshops. In spite of being very rich, they insist on sending their children to state schools, but buy large houses in areas where the state schools will be most populated with middle-class children anyway. Trendy lefties drive round in foreign cars, have colour television and bang on about the evils of consumerism. Conscious of the world population problem, they are thrown into a complete panic if they get pregnant with a third child, and contemplate having an abortion or going to the country to have it, in case other trendy lefties find out.

When you visit them they say: "The kids will be down in a minute," as though a herd of goats is about to come stampeding down the stairs. Their children are bright, but have the most frightful accents, which they pretend not to mind about. They have playrooms rather than nurseries.

They dislike animals but keep neurotic dogs, because they've read somewhere it's good for children to be brought up with animals. They speak with accents, but occasionally forget and when angry or frightened can talk with quite posh voices.

COUNTY LADIES

Summer County, Some are County, some are not.

Upper-class ladies always wear their hair off their foreheads, and their skirts on the knee at exactly the right height to be goosed by large gundogs. Whereupon they say: "He can smell my dog on me."

Upper-class ladies have clean eyes, country-life

45

faces, wear dung-coloured clothes, and can be heard from three acres away. Much of their lives is spent beating bracken, walking hound puppies and displaying large tweed bottoms in the herbacious border. They have houses in Scotland, shotgun honeymoons rather than weddings and all know each other.

Conversation is limited to Dutch elm disease, lake draining, wildlife parks, and the servants who are never in the right house at the right time.

They are not snobbish and the most damning thing they would say about another woman is she's the "Sort of gel who wears shocking pink in the country."

They don't get much sex from their husbands. There is a story about an ancient peer who woke up for the first time in years with an erection.

"Shall we inform her ladyship?" said the butler impassively.

"No, no, Treadwell," said the Earl. "Let's smuggle it down the back stairs and take it up to London."

ZOO-MANIACS:
THANK HEAVEN FOR LITTLE GULLS

Earth-box mothers, who fill their houses with animals, tend to be indifferent to men. They prefer the uncritical adulation of an animal who will never answer back and will adore them whether their hips spread or red veins proliferate on their cheeks.

They usually have houses that smell like the zoo, not a hare out of place, and furniture upholstered in ginger fur. They never wash up, cats' little tongues being far more abrasive than any pan-scourer.

Their motto is love me, love my dugs.

SLUTS

Sluts wash their hair once a month, have goaty armpits, gorgonzola feet, nails filled with eyeshadow, and laundry baskets pulsating like compost heaps.

One slut I knew never washed her pants, only ironed them. You can imagine the steam that rose off that.

When men help them on with their coats they always put their arms down the lining and can't get their coats on.

Herrick as well as hustling virgins has a lot to answer for on the slut front too.

"A sweet disorder in the dress kindles a kind of wantonness," is the slut's motto, and a marvellous excuse for uncombed hair, laddered stockings and dresses welded together with safety pins.

Sluts are always panic-stricken when they lose their bags, not because there's any money in them, but because someone might discover the mass of bus tickets, hair, clogged make-up and 55 mascara brushes inside.

Twice recently where women's magazines have asked if they could photograph the contents of my bag, I've had to go out and buy a new one, and fill it with completely new things. On the most recent occasion I only just stopped my husband filling it with dog biscuits and strange auto-erotic devices.

47

"I regret having to inform you, Miss Gordon, but we have incinerated your underclothing."

Sluts wear their hair over one eye because they're too lazy to pluck both eyebrows, have very weak arms which makes them deficient in elbow grease, and wash up with fingers and cold water or their husband's flannel.

When they get married, and sluts always do because they're quite capable of cleaning themselves up during their courting days, they have houses decorated by runny-nosed brats and unemptied chamber pots.

DOILY BIRDS

Prissy prissy maiden.

Very refined, they come wrapped in cellophane complete with their own pedestal. They always sit in cars like stuck pigs until the driver runs all the way round and lets them out, can't be sworn in front of, and screw their faces into 'neat gin' expressions when people tell filthy jokes.

48

When asked what they'd like to drink they say just a sweet sherry, and when asked if they'd like another one they put their hands over the glass.

When doily birds go to the loo, they rustle paper all the time, lining the seat so that no-one can hear anything. They keep their Tampax in blue plastic holders. They tend to wear Laura Ashley dresses, ribbons in the hair, Peter Pan collars and six pairs of knickers, and talk about fourheads. Their children wear frilly knickers over their plastic pants, and ruched bikini tops at the age of four.

"So important to be feminine," says the doily bird, throwing herself on to her husband's knee, and talking in baby talk.

She also says 'Cos' and 'Comfy' all the time, has a voice like Katie in the Oxo ads, wears colourless nail varnish, and lays a doily under her husband before he gets into bed. She and her husband often call each other Mummy and Daddy.

At mealtimes she serves up aeroplane food, which looks better than it tastes. Everything in the fridge is in plastic containers.

"Foiled again," says the paté dispiritedly to the cheese.

My brother and his wife once had a doily bird to lunch and gave her a mixed grill including a kidney. Too refined to say she didn't like offal, she slipped the kidney into her hand and held it there through the rest of lunch. Finally after lunch they went into the drawing room, and my brother maliciously enjoyed watching her edge towards the fire and when she thought no one was looking

49

flick the kidney into it, whereupon it let off the most terrible hiss.

WOMEN'S LIB LADIES

A Ms is as good as a Male.

One of the most heinous crimes of the twentieth century is to say all Women's Lib Ladies are ugly and Lesbian and only Libbers because they've been hurt and can't get it together with a man. Certainly looking at those brawling aggressive Coven-fresh harpies who attend Women's Lib meetings or represent the movement on television, one would be forgiven for thinking so. While one sympathises with many of their aims, one can only deplore the stridency and violence and whining with which they try to enforce them.

"I tell you Women's Lib needs all the support it can get."

Although they are always agitating for equal pay, they get very uptight if men don't get up when they come into the room or expect them to pay for drinks. They are always complaining about women being exploited as sex objects, but we never hear the sex objects themselves complain.

At parties Sexual Norm, who is suffering from Suffragette Lag, is often asked how he stands on Women's Lib. To which he replies: "I'd like to jump up and down on them."

Men who support Women's Lib actively are always extremely wet.

COSMO GIRLS

The complete antithesis of Women's Lib Ladies. All sex objects, they have bouncing curvy figures, rub baby oil into their bottoms every night, and exercise their vaginal muscles in the bus queue. They are all gourmet cooks, size ten, and produce the same candlelit recipe every month. They read the newspapers every day and are terribly understanding about impotence or premature ejaculation. Most of them are having far too exciting a time in their jobs and being Olympic level in bed, to settle down until they're at least forty. With so many Cosmo girls floating around it's surprising the rest of us ever get a man at all.

SMALL WOMEN

Have a tendency to tweeness, and say "I'm only a

51

little 'un" and make a hell of a row so they don't get lost at parties.

Apart from making one feel like a carthorse by comparison, I've always detested small women since a boy friend, after staring at me for about half an hour, said: "Gosh, you'd be heartbreaking if you were tiny."

"I said, Miss Marriott, there isn't a tall tree that can't be climbed."

TALL GIRLS

Stand about at parties looking gentle and apologetic like Great Danes. Women's magazines are always exhorting them to play up their height with high heels, so they bang their heads on the ceiling, and to wear bold dramatic prints so they can hook bold dramatic princes.

GROUPIES: PHALLUS IN WONDERLAND

A teenage friend tells me that "promiscuous" is a word that doesn't exist any more, because everyone is. Groupies are girls that specialise in sleeping with pop singers, which can't be much fun. They are inhabited rather than inhibited, wear non-stick frying pants and have eyes that don't drop quickly enough but knickers that do.

In America really classy groupies decorate their walls with plaster casts made of their own private parts and the members of famous pop stars they have slept with. Flying Fucks rather than ducks, I suppose.

COUNTRY GIRLS

Have pink cheeks, flat shoes, clean underwear, and an innocent but healthy attitude towards sex, having seen so many animals copulate and give birth. When they visit London they're easy to pick out because they're so much more done up than anyone else.

TOMBOYS

Tomboys have ruffable hair, freckled faces, scarred knees from climbing trees, big nipples, small breasts, and often go as men to fancy dress parties.

"I was a terrible tomboy at school," is the cue for long boring reminiscences about how naughty they were. They refer to their boy friends as "my chap" or "my bloke", and like being spanked for sexual kicks because it recreates the stormy relationship they had with Miss Pickersgill at school.

THE BRICK

A brick is the sort of girl you fall back on rather than forward onto. She's the good sport who doesn't mind being blown to bits in cars, or freezing on the touchline, and is happy to go dutch and drink half pints. She reads the sports pages, and does the *Telegraph* crossword in half an hour, inking out the clues as she goes. The Brick drives her own car, which she lends to men to take out prettier girls, and is always left to do all the cooking when she goes sailing. Men treat her very badly. They often mean it literally when they say in the pub: "I dropped a frightful brick last night."

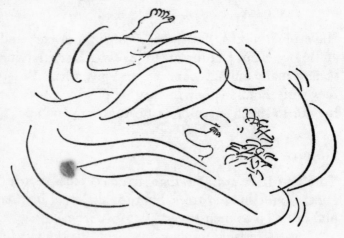

"I say—steady on old girl."

STEADIES

Girls who are going steady walk round with their arms round their boy friends as though they were running in a three-legged race but had forgotten to tie their inside legs together. They spend a lot of time gazing at each other in doorways, and will say, "We go out on Tuesday, Thursday and the week-end." They eat very slowly when they go out, because as they're holding hands they have to cut up their meat with their fork. They are inclined to produce creased photographs of the beloved, and say: "It's a terribly bad one of him."

WOMEN'S WOMEN

"Gosh, there's this marvellous girl at nursery school, Alexander's madly in love with her," raves Honor to Sexual Norm. "She's got a super figure."

Women regard super figures as being thin; and sex appeal as having a pink and white complexion, regular features, a glint-free eye, and being generally wholesome, rather like girls that introduce children's television programmes.

MEN'S WOMEN

Who ever loved that hated not at first sight.

The ideal sex partner gives promise of a good tussle. The more animosity she harbours the better. She is the opulent tigress, the bitch goddess with a 38 bust, a very narrow back and endless legs, the man-hater who is bashed into fawning submission by the hero in the last chapter. Helen of Troy—the most beautiful woman who ever lived—was very fond of wrestling.

BEAUTIES

"May she be granted beauty and yet not,
Beauty to make a stranger's eye distraught,
Or hers before a looking glass . . ."   W. B. YEATS

The beauty has a design-centre sticker on her bottom, and sends men's hands fluttering like butterflies to straighten their ties or smooth their hair whenever she enters a room.

One automatically thinks of Lady Diana Cooper or Polly in *The Pursuit of Love*, the sort of woman one can't stop gazing at in the pathetic hope she might have gone off in the last few seconds.

Most of the beautiful women I know are, most unfairly, extremely intelligent, but somehow they seem to spend so much time primping, looking at themselves in the mirror, going on diets and having stormy affaires that they never seem to do much with their lives. Like Ming vases, they are beautiful but empty. As a result they have frightful hang-ups about being just a pretty face, and the quickest way to get them into bed is to tell them you admire them for their minds.

Most women admire beautiful women and get a certain kudos having them as friends. Women often indulge in pointless conversation about whether people are pretty, sexy, beautiful or attractive, fishing like mad for the other person to say: "Of course you're all four."

MODELS

Models have difficult pregnancies, high tight self-assured bottoms, and moustaches drawn on them in the tube. They are often filmed drifting through the buttercups in a nightie or performing fellatio on a bar of chocolate. They retire at twenty. Most of them have their teeth fixed, so they're capped women rather than kept women, and manage to smile dazzlingly and keep their eyes wide open at the same time. In bed they are like skeletons.

Whenever a man takes a model out he always describes her as a top, never a bottom model. They do not have brains and say y'know, funtastic.

NURSES

Monstering Angels

Nurses are very smug because all their patients think they're absolutely wonderful. They have a profound contempt for anyone outside the medical profession. They always know too much.

Quite unshockable, they prefer men horizontal to vertical. Night nurses are at home all day, and therefore a good bet for married men.

NANNIES

Have a terrible life, living in other people's houses as part of the family, yet not part of it. Every time they try to discipline the children the mother drifts in and messes everything up. Parents assume that Nannies get so frightened of getting fond of the children that they must move on every few months. Actually, they get sick to the teeth of the parents.

57

We've been through every kind of Nanny: the sexy towel-slipping variety, one who ate cheese all day and used to bath in the dark, another who set fire to the drawing-room twice and turned the dog into an alcoholic, another who had black men in all night, another who wanted to be a nun and kept discussing her heavy periods with my unfortunate husband. Another looked like a ferret, and my husband used to make ferret faces behind her back to make me laugh; another ran up fifty pounds of grocery bills on my account.

When I interview them now, after telling them about the colour television in their rooms and the run of the telephone and my husband, I add: "I'd like you to stay at least a week."

CONTINENTAL GIRLS

When I was a gel, foreign girls used to be considered the only people who knew anything about sex, but today English girls have easily outstripped them.

As one Spanish au pair girl said: "When they came to my country I thought, Oh well, they're on holiday letting themselves go a bit. Now I'm in England I see they're like this all the time."

Swedes are supposed to be all sex maniacs, to bath in Badedas and to be Bad for Dad. French girls have an innate sense of superiority: they're like Old Etonians—not necessarily superior, they just think they are. Spaniards have very hairy legs, and however much they shave, bristles stick through their stockings like Mrs Tiggy Winkle.

"On Sunday efeninks eet is elk yoursel'."

Sexual Norm has a German au pair, and keeps them in stitches in the local saying: "The trouble with my house is that it's over krauted."

AMERICAN GIRLS

Hygienic with the light brown hair.

All cheese dipsomaniacs. If you go to drinks with one you'll be prevailed upon to plunge bits of raw carrot and cauliflower into disgusting goo, and given such strong martinis, you'll feel too sick to have any dinner.

Americans are useful at parties because they always say Parm Me when they're introduced to anyone, so you catch the names the second time round.

They regard Europe as dreadfully dirty. "The English have more wax in their ears than they have on their tables," said one American.

59

Most of them are going to analysts, have plastic private parts to withstand a deluge of vaginal deodorants, and go in for Caesarian births:

"To keep your toobes honeymoon fresh."

Older American women—the Blue Rinse Brigade —charge round Europe wearing plaid and plastic concertina headscarfs to keep off the rain, and give cries of anguish at everything old.

A member of the Blue Rinse Brigade and her husband visited an English peeress recently. The husband, who was called Elmer, sat in bootfaced silence during the whole visit, but as they were leaving the wife said "So nice socialising with you, Lady X. I have nev-urr seen El-murr so animated."

Afterwards Lady X went back into the drawing room and found a vast box of chocolates lying on the sofa, as big as the sofa. On top was a card printed with the words:

"To the loveliest lady we know."

American intellectuals differ from English intellectuals, in that as well as being clever, they are often beautiful and extremely good at cooking and running a house. They use so many long words, it is difficult to understand them. They call their bags 'pocket books'.

LESBIANS

Very fashionable at the moment. As a reaction against the coolness and narcissism of the young men today, girls are dressing up in men's suits, cutting their hair short and wearing trilbies like Lulu.

The world is supposed to be teeming with unrecognised Lesbians who look like everyone else. Men are rather keen on the idea, and have fantasies about watching two Lesbians in bed together, but they visualise two lovely young things with trembling golden buttocks, rather than two hoary old frumps with monocles and Eton crops thrashing around like dinosaurs.

Women are often described as Practising Lesbians as though they spent seven hours a day at it, like musicians.

NYMPHOMANIACS

Chaps with Everything—Here comes old Knickerless Nickleby.

Supposed to be Lesbian or frigid, might be very tired and want to lie down all the time, or be doing market research into mattresses.

Nymphomaniacs have for hire signs on their foreheads, mad eyes that look as though they've been swimming under water too long, sandpaper vaginas, and the acceleration of an Aston Martin towards anything in trousers. Their approach is to sidle up and say: "I've got a bottle of whiskey at home."

I used to know a nymphomaniac called the Garrison Bicycle because everyone rode her. She was supposed to be impossible to satisfy and men went off gland in hand into the sunrise.

My husband has always wanted to meet a nymphomaniac; he says the ultimate rejection would be to be turned down by one.

WHORES

All hands to the Pimp—my orifice is my fortune.

Tarts have hearts and parts of gold.

Respectable women kid themselves that prostitutes are all old bags (or American old pocket books) or Lesbians who hate every moment of it. But some of the ones I've met have been ravishingly pretty and were having a high old time.

One man I knew went to bed with a tart in Hamburg and was charged the equivalent of £190. He paid by American Express.

A friend who had a wooden leg was driving down Park Lane before the days of the Wolfenden Report, when an enormous negress put her head through the window and said: "Want to come home with me?"

To which he replied: "What, all the way to bloody Africa?"

TEASERS

Chaste are the ears
Although the eyes are rogues. LA FONTAINE

Teasers grin but don't bear it, they want to attract men and bask in their admiration, but not reap the consequences. They will not sin for their supper.

Prickteasers flirt and tease, chatter and giggle, produce a force-ten gale fluttering their false eyelashes, and are always brushing imaginary crumbs off men's trousers, knowing they have already thrown the keys to their chastity belt in the river.

Prickteasers say "Oh go on," and don't mean it.

"Your oats were in the porridge, Hamish."

SCOTSMEN (see Tory Ladies)

They wear pleated skirts on the knee and their bushes outside. Their wives are full of beans and bairns.

INDIAN LADIES

You undress them by unbandaging them; often they unravel themselves and take nude photographs in instant machines on railway stations. They make disgusting carrot pudding, and always take everything you say seriously.

63

FRIGID WOMEN

She'll be coming round the mountain when she comes— singing Ay Yay Yippy.

With all the books on female sexuality pouring off the presses, I would have thought it was virtually impossible for a woman to be frigid these days. More controversy rages over the location of the female orgasm than ever did over the source of the Nile. Whether you're in the clitoris or the vagina camp, if you don't achieve multiple orgasm every time, you feel one of the flops of the decade.

Like the pathetic letter in *Forum* recently:

"I've never had the smidgeon of an orgasm and sherry doesn't help."

A famous beauty who's kept more lovers happy than I've had hot dinners told me she's always been frigid:

"I just wriggle about and pretend."

People are always saying about frigid women:

"She's got two children, she must have done it twice, ha ha ha ha."

Frigid women who have saved it for marriage are determined not to spend it all at once. They dawdle over their baths, and are horrified when they read in sex books that lots of men are still leading vigorous lives in their eighties.

It seems a pity, if you don't like sex, that you can't hire someone to sleep with your husband. After all you employ a Nanny to look after your children, which is one of the traditional wifely functions.

NEUROTICS

Valium is the better part of discretion.

PIN-UP GIRLS

"You must not forget the suspenders, best beloved." KIPLING

Gatefold nudes have staples through their stom-achs, are the colour of Red Indians, have double-barrelled names like Mary Blanche-Maison, live in Sussex and read Greek at Oxford.

Pin-ups are usually photographed in high heels, stockings and suspender belts, jewelry, big hats and newly set hair, as though they were arriving at a smart society wedding, but had forgotten to put on their dresses. Although they often appear to be lying down, they are in fact photographed against a wall so their breasts don't go fe-lop. If they are photo-graphed with pubic hair it's known in the trade as beaver; if they have their legs apart it's called split beaver, which upsets both Mary Whitehouse and the R.S.P.C.A.

OLDER WOMEN

*"No spring nor summer beauty has such grace
As I have seen in one autumnal face."* DONNE

When I was a teenager I thought middle age started at thirty, but as I get older it starts later and later, as the end of one's shadow gets further and further away as nightfall approaches. Ever since my thirty-

c

first birthday I've got out of bed every morning, peered at my naked body in the mirror and said, not bad for nearly forty.

Older women spend too much time looking for liver spots on their hands, and crêpe on their thighs, and wondering whether they ought to cut their hair short, buy an all-in-one foundation garment, start making love in the dark, and turning off lights and sitting with their backs to the window.

They also try very hard to be gooder and have a better sense of humour because it's supposed to show in one's face after forty.

What is the older woman's role in life? Does one give up sex altogether, or will one's future be initiating shy schoolboys and boy scouts into the mysteries of mature love? They're so precocious these days, they're all having each other at twelve anyway.

The most important thing is not to be a nuisance. Ageing women who throw themselves at men imagining they're still young and beautiful are like my dog after he's swum in the muddy river or rolled in manure, who then bounds up expecting everyone to pet and adore him just the same.

It seems sad that society disapproves so strongly of women having affairs with younger men. I suppose it all stems from the ability to produce children. After forty a woman is not likely to provide her young lover with lusty sons, whereas the older man is perfectly capable of giving a lovely young thing a baby up to the age of eighty.

Women and their Pastimes

HOUSEWORK

The call of the running tidier.
The glory that is elbow grease.

Few tasks are more like the tortures of Sissy-fuss than housework, the clean being made dirty, the dirty clean. Houseproud ladies spend their lives ferreting out fluff from under beds, sponging fingerprints off their husbands, and moving ashtrays half a degree nor-nor-west. They also have Jay cloths permanently at the ready. All they think about in the Spring is cleaning, and when you hear them having intense discussions about fast coloureds and delicate whites they're talking about their washing machines not about sex.

Nowhere does Parkinson's Law operate so efficiently as in the house: mechanical gadgets don't cut down the time spent, they just mean you wash sweaters after you've worn them once instead of scraping the food blob off with your fingernail, and that you feel honour bound to make mayonnaise in the mixer rather than getting it out of a bottle.

Most housewives, Women's Lib tell us, work an eighty-hour week, and therefore get slightly irritated when people say:

"What do you do?"

"I'm a housewife."

"What do you *do* with yourself all day?"

Or when their husbands say smugly "Oh my wife doesn't work."

Their status is consequently sustained by a spotless kitchen and by raising housework to an art form.

"Get off Roger—the sheets were changed this morning."

The whole scene is fraught with problems. On the one hand you read magazine articles warning you that the battle against decay is a denial of life, and that marriages break up because wives are always flapping dusters. Or that children's lives are very short, and how glad you'll be you let the washing-up pile up that Wednesday and spent all day making doll's clothes.

On the other hand you have vague worries, as you trip over a child's bicycle in the hall or look at your toy and nappy strewn kitchen, about the Greek love of order and beauty, and how men loathe muddle, and that behind every really successful man is a clockwork wife.

I think women do all that sighing and ferocious tidying and banging about of pans at weekends to show their husbands how hard they work and because they're panic-stricken that the place won't be tidy enough when the char turns up on Monday morning.

GOSSIPING

Here comes lovely Mrs Cooper—the soul of indiscretion.

Women seem to find it necessary to spend half the day on the telephone talking at 10,000 words a minute to their friends. Men get furious when their wives gossip on the telephone: "You get so silly," complains my husband.

He also gets wildly irritated when I closet myself with female relations on family weekends and indulge in the usual indignation meetings:

"High time that dog went to prep school . . . and what about Uncle Tom's Cabin boy . . . so selfish of Alison to have only one, large families bring each other up." (Like cannibals, I suppose.)

TONGUE CLICKING

Another favourite hobby is clicking the tongue, pursing lips and poking one's nose into other people's business. Old crones in fawn herring-bone coats do it individually, shivering the net curtains every time you go out without a bra or talk to anyone who isn't your husband; or throwing up windows and complaining every time you give noisy parties.

Angry Mothers, a collective body much publicised by the newspapers, are always working up states of fury and clicking their tongues over the school lavatories: "These toilets are disgusting . . . definitely."

69

"George, but how do you know the fridge light goes off when the door shuts?"

WORRYING

Women are not happy unless they've got something to worry about, usually the size of their bust, or losing their looks. If more than one woman are gathered together with rapt expressions on their faces and slightly watering mouths, they're talking about:

SLIMMING

"There will be too much of me in the coming by and by."
W. S. GILBERT

'Flu and falling in love are the only ways to lose weight, both a bit of a nuisance if you've got a husband and children.

"I eat sensibly," says Super Woman, "I watch my figure."

Honor eats insensibly. Two drinks and she doesn't care any more: "Must have something to blot up the alcohol," she says, diving for the canapés.

Next morning the Woman's Page will be advocating post-holiday slimming diets because they've got nothing else to write about. And Honor will be aware of her trouser zips plummeting and seams splitting. She will vow not to buy any more cheap clothes, and

70

wonder if her trousers could possibly have shrunk at the cleaners. She then leans backwards and forwards on the scales to make them weigh lighter, does her trousers up with a safety pin which gives more leeway than a hook and eye, and wishes nostalgically she'd lived in Edwardian days when our great grandfathers drooled over fleshy ladies.

One of the difficulties of going on a diet is the revolting things you have to eat—grapefruit without

"Well the lettuce may be out of the garden but it's by every cat in Barnes."

sugar, vegetables without butter, and undressed lettuce. It's no wonder you feel very bad-tempered and think about food the whole time.

Anyway fatness per se isn't unattractive, it's just the voluminous black sweaters, and tunic tops, and heavily made-up face to detract from the blocky figure, that is.

As soon as Honor loses weight she starts wearing all the clothes she looked too fat in before she lost weight, and so looks exactly the same.

THIN WOMEN

I eat like a horse.

Nothing is more irritating than thin women who are always going on diets.

"Can't get into any of my clothes," they say, ribs pushing through their unisex blouses. "I just cut out potatoes if I gain a few pounds."

The Cosmopolitan Doctor, who can't enter into any correspondence, says latent homosexuals go for very thin girls like Twiggy, and men who are looking for their mothers go for fat girls. So take your pick.

SHOPPING

Nothing brings out the gladiatorial spirit more in women. They make out ludicrous shopping lists: 3 spanish navels, 2 Comforts, 1 large Pal, 2 small Chum, one Tom pureé, then disappear into vast chain-stores and ferociously crash their steel trolleys against one another.

God knows why they're called supermarkets, as there's nothing super about them. One spends far more than one intends to and by the time some pink-overalled crone has finished jabbing away at an adding machine one discovers one hasn't enough money for everything.

When middle-aged ladies come to London, they

head straight for Marshalls, and have lunch with their daughters, who work as "sekketries". Believing their daughters never eat properly in London, they force on them a vast meal of a glass of sherry, tomato soup, plaice fried in breadcrumbs, fruit salad and white coffee.

Afterwards, the glass of sherry having gone to their heads, the mothers buy several good wool or 'semi-evening' dresses, come home absolutely exhausted with too many carrier bags and say they could never live in London. They then hide the carrier bags, and bring out one new dress a week to show their husbands, lying about the price.

CLOTHES

Men never quite understand why clothes are so important to women. "What does it matter what you wear?" says my husband, after at least six dresses have been tried on. "No one's going to look at you anyway."

"That's what I'm afraid of," I mutter.

Women buy most of what shows off the best part of their anatomy. Women with good legs spend a fortune on shoes, those with good busts spend fortunes on sweaters. Before I married I used to buy a new dress every week; it was considered death to romance to be seen in the same thing twice.

Jackie Onassis used to spend £16,000 a week on her clothes. Onassis was absolutely delighted when with superhuman effort she cut down to £8000 a week.

73

HATS

Women put on special faces when they try on hats, pursing up their mouths and opening their eyes very wide.

When I was seventeen I remember changing in the school train to meet a boy friend to go to *South Pacific*. I wore a pair of grey suede shoes, a bright emerald-green coat, and a black straw hat with a veil and a red rose on the front like a miner's lamp.

We had lunch in a Chinese restaurant, and I had great difficulty eating through the veil—bits of Chop Suey kept getting stuck.

Everyone stared at me, I remember, and I assumed it was because I looked smashing, but it must have been because I looked such a fright. As is the case with most hats, you get stared at rather than fancied.

In Yorkshire there's a saying 'Red hat, no knickers,' which always cheers one up when one sees a bossy Tory lady in a red pull-on felt. Poke bonnets are worn by girls who want to get poked.

SEAMSTRESSES

Women spend a lot of time and *angst* dressmaking. I used to come home and find pieces of stuff all over the floor, and my mother with her mouth full of pins talking exactly like John Wayne. Quite often she would cut out two left fronts. By the time she had finished the garment, she was usually so bored, and my father was so bombed with: "It does look all right, doesn't it darling?" that neither of them could ever look at it again.

*"If it was all right for me,
it's all right for you, Griselda—
anyway the forties are back
in fashion."*

Occasionally she would make clothes for me which
caused frightful arguments as she would never make
things tight enough in case my bottom or bust stuck
out too much.

DROPPERS IN

Women have numerous ways of amusing themselves.
One is dropping in—rolling up at nine o'clock in
the morning with the baby and the dog and the
carrycot for a gossip, then standing round watching
you do housework, so you have to wash the glasses in
separate water and can't taste the cooking too much,
or blow your nose on a drying-up cloth.

Others turn up with a bag of maggoty windfalls,
say how's the babe and try and rope you in for what
my son calls 'jungle sales'. These women are usually

75

"It may *be a fine time to drop in, Mummy, but actually I've dropped out."*

described as saints, which means they have big feet, and never wear make-up or bitch about people. Saints tend to have large families of sons who hug them in the kitchen and say: "You're the only woman in my life, Mum."

They go to early service on Sunday then ring you at 8.30 when you're in the middle of making love, saying: "Sorry to bother you so early, but I knew you'd be up, having children."

COFFEE MORNINGS

Women also feel it is important to get on with each other during the day, so they give coffee mornings, which are sheer purgatory—cocktail parties without sex or drink. After coffee and gâteaux you discuss a book you've all read, recommend time-saving products to one another, discuss baby's difficult bottom and play word games.

One woman was asked to think up the name of a

part of the body named after an animal. The answer was actually Hare, but she was thrown out for writing down Pussy.

HOLIDAYS

When women go on holiday, even for a day trip to Boulogne, they spend three weeks packing and buying up the entire local chemist because they don't trust any of those foreign medicines. Rows occur at sporadic intervals, after Honor's ruptured the bathroom scale with her excess baggage, or, if they're travelling by car, because Sexual Norm refuses to stop on the endless autoroutes for anything but petrol.

When they finally reach their destination, Honor is irritated that all her crease-free dresses have creased, and her Carmen rollers and her travelling iron won't fit into any of the sockets.

That night Honor goes out in her holiday uniform of a sleeveless dress and a white cardigan and expresses horror at all those little children drinking wine. Next morning she spends even longer getting ready for the beach than she would for a ball. By evening she has had too much sun, and all she wants to do after two bottles of wine at dinner is to go to bed at 10.30. This happens most nights of the holiday but she still grumbles because Norm, irritated by not getting enough sex, hot foots off to the casino every evening and blues all their savings buying whiskey at 100 francs a tot for some French tart.

As the holiday goes on, Honor looks permanently

as though she's just come out from under the dryer, and she has to wear looser and looser flowered orlon tops to conceal her spreading hips. She and Norman have also met up with an English couple and both couples feel honour bound to retire to bed for three hours every afternoon in case the other couple should think them undersexed.

Honor lies on the beach and wishes she could have a slim brown figure like those French girls reading *Elle*. She wishes she hadn't had three croissants for breakfast, and vows to skip lunch. Then she sees all those slim brown girls tucking into great loaves of bread and salad niçoise and decides to have some too.

"Just think! In 24 hours it's home and half a grapefruit a day only, for the next three months."

The way to *Elle* is paved with good intentions.

Before they go home Honor and Norm have a row because Honor wants to spend the rest of their money buying presents for the children, her daily woman and her mother, and Norm wants to spend it on the tart at the casino.

SKIING

Occasionally women go skiing, come back glowing with health and clean up at winter cocktail parties, because everyone else is the colour of bacon fat. As soon as the men get them home and rip off their clothes, they discover these girls are also the colour of bacon fat except for their faces, and lose interest. To try and win them back, the girls give revolting Glühwein parties, show slides, and try to re-create the atmosphere of the châlet.

OLD GIRLS

People who go back to old girls' reunions were usually in the hockey eleven or prefects for whom the world never recovered its magic after they left school. Everyone is very hectic, they all blow in and out, and rock the room with gales of laughter and reminisce about jokes in the dorm and the crush everyone had on Miss Pickersgill.

Honor, who was not a success at school, looks at all her contemporaries and secretly hopes she doesn't look as old as that. They are all doing the same to her.

She finds herself talking just as obsequiously to the muscle-bound frump who was captain of hockey, as she ever did when she was at school.

Looking around at the eager unpainted faces, the whispy hair, the baggy skirts, she's amazed so many of them have married. The uniform seems to be lots of cardigans, fur-lined boots, an inch of petticoat showing beneath the skirt, and a large beret of neutral-coloured felt pulled down to one side.

GREAT GIRL FRIENDS

Women spend hours talking to their friends on the telephone saying How's so and so, he's fine, and how's so and so, and she's fine, and how's etc. etc. She's a *great* girl friend of mine, they say, so you imagine some huge amazon walking through the door. Women like women for different reasons than men do: they can get very attached to humorous boots, girls at work, girls next door with whom they can discuss nappies and the price of fish, none of whom are likely to appeal to their husbands.

Honor finds she has to smuggle in the friends Norman doesn't like. "Marion might just possibly pop over after lunch on Sunday," means she's actually invited Marion to dinner.

When pretty friends come to stay, Norm is very accommodating, and only too happy to fix their bedroom light after everyone else has gone to bed, take them early morning tea, and drive them to the airport.

Intense loyalty to one's girl friends is an excellent let-out when you don't fancy the husband:

"Oh I couldn't possibly do it to Honor," cries Honor's best friend.

Norman, who has fantasies about three in a bed and both of them doing it to Honor, is very disappointed.

When women want to escape from each other at parties or in the street they say: "We must have lunch sometime."

"No, I bloody well won't point the car in the direction of the map!"

WOMEN IN CARS

Young girls generally kick their shoes off when they drive cars, say 'sugar' when they grind the gears, and tend to go forward in a succession of jerks. If they go to a party in their car and meet an attractive man, they pretend they've come in a taxi on the chance of getting a lift home. A pounce is worth a parking ticket.

They regard cars rather like washing machines, and deliberately refuse to take any interest in what goes on underneath the bonnet.

Men fancy girls in sports cars, but dislike being driven by them except when it means missing valuable drinking time.

How often at a party you see a woman sourly sipping tomato juice and the husband happily swilling whiskey "because Jennifer's driving".

HOSTESSES

Let us now prise out famous men.

As opposed to great girl friends, hostesses are always

described as "little". They have at home cards
printed with their names on so they can just add the
date, write down what they gave people last time,
and invite names to meet names, who never ask them
back.

Once upon a time before the advent of Robert
Carrier and Elizabeth David, one could go out to
dinner and not die of indigestion and hangover the
next day. Now it's all gourmet cooking, cheese
before fruit, three different kinds of wine and wafer-
thin mints.

Norm thinks it's called Cor-may cooking, because
he always says, "Cor, may I have some more." He
describes Honor as a Cordon Bleu cook, which is a
euphemism for any old tat served up with so much
cream and wine and garlic in everything you wake
up burping at three o'clock in the morning.

Super Woman takes half an hour to give a dinner
party. The silver and the plates are all clean anyway
and she has only to whisk five courses out of the deep
freeze, or whip up a quick suprême de leftovers.

Honor takes two days, most of which are spent
racking her brains over the placement, which she
used to think was some kind of liver. Can you have
two queers sitting next to each other, and does a
mistress take precedence over a catamite?

She is so anxious not to have a last-minute panic
that she cooks everything hours ahead. Norm is
sulking because he can't have a bath, the bath being
full of ice cubes. Honor changes into her hostess gown,
the sleeves of which trail in the gravy.

The guests arrive. She has left at least three-quarters of an hour for drinking before dinner, and only a quarter of an hour has gone and Norman's boss's wife, who doesn't drink, is already looking bored. Norm's friend One Night Stan has arrived drunk and is already telling dirty stories.

*"Ronald, don't mention the béarnaise again—
there will be savoury scrambled
eggs for pudding!"*

After two gins and tons, in spite of cooking ahead, Honor is desperately trying to uncurdle a last-minute sauce, keep the toast, now the consistency of flannel, hot, light the candles, and remember to put out the butter and open bottles. Norman having read somewhere that either the host or hostess should stay with the guests, is sticking resolutely to the drawing room.

Honor, who knows a gracious hostess makes a relaxed party, is trying to prise a jammed crust out of the toaster. A smell of burning fills the house.

Now they sit down to dinner, everyone sticking elbows into the next-door neighbour's eyes whenever they help themselves. Norm's boss is getting very excited over One Night Stan's wife, but no one is talking to Norman's boss's wife, who is looking boot-

WOMEN AND SUPER WOMEN

faced. Honor jerks her head to the right, hoping everyone will turn and talk to the guest on their right, but no one does, so she does it again and again, and succeeds in cricking her neck.

The beef, which has been cooking in Châteauneuf du Pape for 12 hours, is completely tasteless. Guests push it to the side of their plates saying 'That grapefruit really filled me up.' Later they fall upon the cheese.

Norman, having cracked his head on the lowslung Christopher Wray lamp last time he got to his feet, is refusing to fill up anyone's glass.

Everyone suddenly jumps out of their skin, at the pneumatic drill shriek of the coffee grinder.

Honor gets graciously to her feet.

"Shall we go upstairs?" she says to the ladies.

"Yes please," says One Night Stan leaping to his feet and following her.

SEX

"To make love without feeling a particle is sad work and sad and serious did I find it."

"Everything's getting on top of me these days except Henry."

Hot on the trail of gourmet cooking comes gourmet sex. Today people start getting hang-ups if they don't have sex beautifully served up three times a day with a piece of parsley on top.

Honor wakes up on Sunday and wearily ticks off all the things that have to be done:

(1) Norman
(2) The children's breakfast
(3) The ironing
(4) The dog's breakfast
(5) Sunday lunch
(6) Norman

It amazes me how couples with young children ever make love at all. Thank God for *Catweazle* or *Doctor Who*, which at least gives you a clear childfree half hour. It should be re-christened family screwing time.

Honor, worried about hers and Norm's sex life and making heroic attempts to improve it, has been reading a book called *How to Improve your Man in Bed*, which tells her she must practise removing Norman's clothes "without clumsiness or hold-ups and preferably with one hand". But who does she practise on?

She is also told to acquire some sexy underclothes. She buys a garter suspender belt which slides down over her bottom the moment she puts it on and makes her new black stockings wrinkle. Another suggestion is to treat Norm to a strip show. She removes her bra as they're going to bed, and waves it round like a football rattle. Norm asks her if she's been at the gin.

Norm is even more worried when Honor, again acting on the advice of *How to Improve your Man in Bed*, moves in the builders to knock down the bedroom wall so they can have a bathroom adjacent to the bedroom, and "not lose any sexual heat running down long cold passages". The builders are shortly followed by the painters to re-decorate the bedroom in more intimate sexy colours. The bill is staggering,

85

"Right—Catweazle, Treasure Island, Dr Who and then Golden Shot and not a sound for the next two hours."

and there are more bills for Honor's school-girl outfit from Daniel Neals, a new double bed, and a huge looking-glass for the ceiling. Norm always believes if you take care of the penis, the pounds will take care of themselves.

Other hints on lovemaking include:

"Tying each other up." (Norman feels Honor bound and then goes off to the pub.) "Throw his pyjamas in the dustbin." Norm is livid, his pyjamas were new, black with red piping, and what's he going to walk round in now when his mother-in-law comes to stay?

"Never tell him Jim was better. Get all dolled up for an evening and tell him you've forgotten your pants." (Norm is horrified and tells Honor to go upstairs and put them on again.)

"Offer to fellate him at odd moments of the day." (She'll get a clip over the ear if it's during "Match of the Day".)

"Make the most of morning erections, but eat apples first to sweeten the breath." (Poor Norman is

86

woken from deep sleep by frenzied fiddling and scrunching, and grumbles he prefers his alarm clock.)

Honor gives up, throws *How to Improve Your Man in Bed* in the dustbin with one hand and goes back to the missionary position once a week.

In Victorian times, women were disapproved of if they enjoyed sex; today they feel guilty if they don't want it all the time. Sex is often the loveliest thing in the world, but people shouldn't feel guilty about having too much or too little. And feeling you ought is just as oppressive as feeling you oughtn't.

THE DATE

"Is it one of my well looking days, child? Am I in face?"
GOLDSMITH

At last One Night Stan rings. Sexual Norma, who has been biting her nails for weeks, drops her voice three octaves and says Hello. Stan asks her out, she says she might be able to squeeze him in, what about Monday, Tuesday, Wednesday, Thursday or Friday? After she puts the telephone back her voice reverts to normal and she shrieks: "He's rung, he's rung."

She then goes out and buys a completely new set of clothes, including a new pair of jeans and a bra to look as though she's not wearing a bra.

On the day of the date, she spends three hours at the hairdressers. When a mirror is held up so she can see the back of her head, she mutters gosh, yes, marvellous. When she gets home she brushes it all out.

She then spends another three hours getting ready,

rouging her navel, washing her ears and spraying scent onto her pulse spots, including the back of her knees.

The doorbell goes. She doesn't feel quite the million dollars she had hoped. A maddening piece of hair keeps sticking out at right angles, mascara has got into her eyes, her jeans, in spite of a 24 hour crash diet, are making her walk two inches off the ground, and even with layers and layers of Erace, a large spot on her nose is shining through like a lighthouse.

"Where shall we eat?" says One Night Stan when he arrives.

Sexual Norma can't think of anywhere except Claridges or Jo Lyons.

The next four hours are spent sipping cocktails, which go straight to Norma's head and other parts of her anatomy, dining by candlelight, dancing in a discothèque blacker than great Agrippa's inkwell, and groping in a taxi on the way back to Norma's flat.

Norma, who is feeling sick through too much drink, wonders if she asks Stan up whether she'll ever get rid of him.

"Would you like a nightcap?" she says timidly.

"Never wear them," says Stan, pushing his way resolutely into the flat.

They then express a mutual interest in gramophone records, and Norma plays a record which she likes because she knows it, but Stan doesn't like because he doesn't know it. One really shouldn't on the first date, says Norma to herself rushing into the bathroom, cleaning her teeth, drenching her bosom in 100 per cent proof, and putting an intellectual French novel by the bed instead of Barbara Carthorse.

Back in the drawing room, Stan puts his hand over Norma's, she puts her other hand over his, he puts his other hand over hers, Norma pulls out her bottom hand to put over his, and this goes on faster and faster until they are slapping each other's hands.

In the bedroom Stan starts to undress her, Norma complies—anything to get out of these crotch-murdering jeans.

Norma doesn't enjoy much of what follows; she tries to remember what *The Sensuous Woman* told her, but all she feels is her mother standing at the end of the bed waving an admonishing finger.

Afterwards she wonders how long she has to lie in simulated ecstasy before charging off to the loo.

When she returns One Night Stan is dressed and about to disappear into the night. For the first time that evening, Norma feels she'll mind very much if she doesn't see him again, and shouts after him, "You will ring me, won't you?"

Of course, he doesn't. Norma's flatmates sympathise with her, but in private they are delighted. They know men. It's all champagne and fairy tales until they've had their all, then you can't see them for dust.

LOVE
"I said to Heart, 'how goes it?' Heart replied:
'Right as a Ribstone Pippin!' But it lied." HILAIRE BELLOC

From smug middle age, it is very easy to be a little

patronising about the agonies of being in love. Often when waiting to hear whether something I've written is going to be accepted, I recapture all the ghastly twitchy uncertainty of a life ruled by the telephone. You know the sort of thing.

He said he'd ring in the morning and now it's five past one, perhaps he's cooling off. And three other men have rung and had their heads bitten off for not being him. And I've just had a cold bath in case I might not hear the telephone over the sound of the geyser. And just rung up the engineer for the third time to see if the telephone's working. Why the hell can't he telephone me so I can stop thinking about him?

Conversely, the moment you go off a man he's never off the bloody blower making a nuisance of himself.

Then there's the agonising rat race of getting men to marry you. As a girl friend of mine screamed at her boy friend the other day: "You haven't even given me a ring that I can give back to you." Or another girl I know who was walking her boy friend purposefully past a jeweller's window, when he paused suddenly and peered inside, his eyes lighting on a large and beautiful ring.

"I like that," he said gazing into her eyes. "Don't you, darling? Do you think we can afford it?"

"Oh, yes, darling," she said, trying to control her ecstasy.

He then went into the shop—and bought the ring for himself.

Then an affair breaks up, and one has to cope with one's friends in a state of uncontrollable misery.

"You'll get over it," you say feebly as though the sodden lump on the sofa was about to undertake the Olympic high jump.

One girl I remember going on and on all evening about how miserable she was, like a rat in a trap: "I love him," I heard her saying dramatically to my husband, "I love him per se."

"Who the hell's Percy," said my husband irritably, "I thought you were in love with someone called Paul."

PARTIES

We are three girls, we share a *flap*.

At girls' parties there are always too many men, at men's parties far too many women. "But you've invited ten extra girls," I wail to my husband.

"Doesn't matter," he says airily. "I can chat up at least five at once and so can Paul."

Girls in flats give parties either because they want to pay back all the men who've wined and dined them, or more usually because they want an excuse to invite a man they've always fancied but never got anywhere with. All the invitations go through the office franking machine, candles are rammed into bottles, and the sort of wine you wouldn't wash your car down with, is served.

If it's a cocktail party, all the men arrive first straight from work at 6.30, and you suddenly have 42 men and two girls. The girls who have gone home to change and tart up don't arrive until eight o'clock, by which time all the men have got bored and gone off with each other or to another party.

If you give an after-dinner party, all the women arrive about 9.30, so you have 42 women and two queers making overbright conversation, until the men arrive after the pubs are closed at 11 o'clock, often bringing girls with them. And finally your best friend goes off with the man who was the reason you gave the party.

ADULTERY

One crowded hour of glorious wife is worth an age without a name.

"For my part, when all's said and done I'd still rather be cuckolded than dead." VOLTAIRE

ALL WORK AND NO PLAY MAKES JACK ADULTEROUS.

I'd prefer not to know, says the reasonable husband. I'll kill you if you look at another man, says the chauvinist pig. The cuckolds in between—the majority —simply don't believe it.

Helen of Troy—a well known adulteress—allowed her husband Menelaus to wine and dine Paris for nine days. Under Menelaus' nose, Paris wrote "I love you" in wine on the table, seized Helen's cup and drank from the same part of it as she did, making sheep's eyes at her, and generally behaving in a very adolescent way. The moment Menelaus was out of the house, Helen pushed off with Paris, abandoning her nine-year-old daughter, who might have grown into competition later, but taking her baby son, several of the palace treasures, gold to the value of five talents and five of the serving maids. Last week, Honor's friend Diana went off with the dentist and the furniture. So times haven't changed.

Adulteresses of today always tell their husband they've been shopping in Knightsbridge, when he comes home in the evening and enquires why they weren't in when he rang.

"I tried on lots of things," they say airily, "but I couldn't find anything that fitted."

Adulteresses get home very late and flustered, and have to placate the au pair with bunches of flowers. Au pairs often have bedrooms like funeral parlours.

Adulteresses gaze at their lovers for hours in parked cars, find they can't book into hotels together unless they've got luggage, and out of opening hours spend a lot of time sitting in residence lounges drinking black coffee and saying No to trolleys of cakes. Even in Paris, hotels with three stars pretend to be puritanical to force the adulterer into booking a second room.

Honor is not very good at being unfaithful to Norm. One day she planned to leave the children with a friend, who suddenly found she couldn't take them. Honor then rang up her lover to cancel lunch and found he had booked a table in another name, and there were five Browns and four Smiths with booked tables.

When she arranges a home fixture, the window-cleaner keeps turning up and grinning at every window.

Women when they start an affair improve enormously in looks; their eyes shine, and their coat gleams as though they've just taken a course of Bob Martins.

"You should have seen her before I moved in," says the lover complacently.

Adultery has become very fashionable these days. It's now called extra-marital sex, and is regarded as a form of therapy: she'll perk up if she has a stint in another man's bed. Jealousy is very out of fashion, but there are an awful lot of bitten nails about.

WIFE SWAPPING

Everyone suddenly burst out swinging.

Wife swapping always seems to happen to other people. London says it all goes on in the country with reference to the hunting shires, the country says of course, it all happens in London; and both London and the country believe it all goes on in the suburbs with wall-to-wall housewives thrumming with lust.

Wife swapping seems so divorced from the caprices of genuine desire. Why should Norma be offered as a sacrificial lamb to another husband just because her husband fancies his wife?

There was a riveting piece in *Over 21* in which a married woman said: "Wife swapping is a sort of phase everyone goes through like pottery and golf. We're not bored with each other, just bored with the set-up. I think women who go round sleeping with other people's husbands in private are much worse."

"Well, it's been quite lovely meeting you Mr & Mrs Hartman but our baby-sitter gets quite upset if we're not back by ten."

In fact the wife swappers are just as prudish and rule-bound as everyone else. Norm for example can sleep with Gideon's wife, and Gideon can sleep with Honor when they're all together, but Norm isn't allowed to slope over to Gideon's wife in the afternoon for a quick bit on the side when the others aren't about.

Once you are a wife swapper, you are also supposed to keep quiet about it, and not tell any one in the outside world, as it will be bad for all the wife swappers' reputations. A sort of Honor among thieves, says Norm.

If there's a wife swapping session on a council estate or in a village, the wife always plays at home in case the children wake up.

How does the whole thing start?

According to *Over 21*:

95

"Usually people ring up and say come round for dinner—and you know what it means. Generally we start with drinks and a buffet supper" (everyone presumably starts buffeting into everyone else) and people disappear upstairs.

"Sometimes the host just says, well let's get on with it. But I do prefer something to eat and drink first. You can have four different men a night if you want to, but if you get sick of it, you just dress and chat, if you don't fancy anyone you needn't join it."

But imagine the Mammoth sulks if Honor refuses Gideon and five minutes later is found thrashing on a mattress with One Night Stan. And how awful if no-one wanted you. And what would one wear, instant tan all over I suppose, and something loose enough not to leave crease marks on your body when you stripped off. And would people start gossiping if you stayed with the same man all night?

Honor, ever loyal, tells the others:

"Norm's frightfully light on his elbows."

TROILISM

Tweedledum and Tweedledee agreed to have a battle-axe.